"Betrayal in churches today. *My Spouse Was Unfaithful* p—compassionate guidance for those walking the painful path of heartbreak, deceit, and hurt. This book offers sufferers hope, helping us wisely navigate this raw and vulnerable situation by pointing us toward God's sovereignty."

Shauna Van Dyke, Strategic Advisor, The Association of Biblical Counselors

"*My Spouse Was Unfaithful* was written by a biblically saturated pastor who knows how to use the Word of God to minister to others. It is full of honesty, truth, and practical help. This book will guide you on how to both recover and grow to be more Christlike and will also be a useful tool for counselors."

Ernie Baker, Pastor of Counseling Supervision and Equipping, First Baptist Church, Jacksonville, FL; chairman of the online BA in Biblical Counseling, The Master's University; author of *Marry Wisely, Marry Well*

"Robert Jones, in this wise and compassionate work, helps us traverse the searing pain of marital infidelity. He reminds us that God's grace and God's truth can sustain us in the hardest times. A valuable work both for those suffering from infidelity and those counseling them."

Thomas R. Schreiner, James Buchanan Harrison Professor of New Testament Interpretation and Associate Dean, The Southern Baptist Theological Seminary

"When your spouse has betrayed you, you will be disoriented and overwhelmed. Robert's short book is a wise companion that will be a reliable guide into God's heart for you."

Edward T. Welch, Faculty and counselor, The Christian Counseling & Educational Foundation (CCEF)

"*My Spouse Was Unfaithful* is a timely, encouraging, and thoughtful text on walking through the aftermath of adultery. Robert Jones brings his decades of counseling experience to bear in this book, providing a concrete, gospel-centered, and Christ-honoring approach to responding to infidelity. It is filled with biblical wisdom that seeks to understand the unique struggles of each individual while bringing true Hope to believers. It's a must-read for anyone counseling others through this struggle."

Kristin Kellen, Associate Director of EdD Studies and Associate Professor of Biblical Counseling, Southeastern Baptist Theological Seminary

"In the moments after adultery, we scarcely envision a day when marriage can be restored, not to what it was, but to something more, to something only the grace and power of the gospel can accomplish. Robert Jones shows how the Lord Jesus helps you take wise, faith-filled steps in restoring a marriage broken by adultery. I gladly commend this resource to you."

John Henderson, Associate Professor of Biblical Counseling, The Southern Baptist Theological Seminary; associate pastor, University Baptist Church; author of *Catching Foxes*

MY SPOUSE WAS UNFAITHFUL

FINDING STRENGTH
IN GOD'S PRESENCE

Robert D. Jones

New
Growth
Press

newgrowthpress.com

New Growth Press, Greensboro, NC 27401
newgrowthpress.com
Copyright © 2023 by Robert D. Jones

Cover Design: Studio Gearbox, studiogearbox.com
Interior Typesetting and eBook: Lisa Parnell, lparnellbookservices.com

ISBN: 978-1-64507-387-1 (Print)
ISBN: 978-1-64507-388-8 (eBook)

Library of Congress Cataloging-in-Publication Data
Names: Jones, Robert D., 1959– author.
Title: My spouse was unfaithful : finding strength in God's presence / Robert D. Jones.
Description: Greensboro, NC : New Growth Press, [2023] | Series: Ask the Christian counselor | Summary: "Provides practical and accessible biblical guidance for dealing with the betrayal of adultery and moving forward with God-given hope"— Provided by publisher.
Identifiers: LCCN 2023019281 (print) | LCCN 2023019282 (ebook) | ISBN 9781645073871 (Print) | ISBN 9781645073888 (e-book)
Subjects: LCSH: Adultery—Biblical teaching. | Marriage—Religious aspects—Christianity. | Spouses—Religious life. | Church work.
Classification: LCC BV4627.A3 J659 2023 (print) | LCC BV4627.A3 (ebook) | DDC 248.8/44—dc23/eng/20230602
LC record available at https://lccn.loc.gov/2023019281
LC ebook record available at https://lccn.loc.gov/2023019282

Printed in the United States of America

30 29 28 27 26 25 24 23   1 2 3 4 5

Dedication

I am grateful to the many men and women who have allowed me, as your pastor or as an outside counselor, to enter your life after suffering some form of marital infidelity. You privileged me by letting me weep with you and bring the light of God's Word into your dark places. Thank you. You have reminded me (and my co-counselors who assisted us) of the empowering grace of God, and you have demonstrated a remarkable love for Christ that has encouraged and inspired my own faith in our Savior.

CONTENTS

Chapter 1

MOVING FORWARD
WITH GOD-GIVEN HOPE[1]

How do we deal with the devastating disappointments that infidelity brings? One response is vengeful anger, mirroring the country song about a woman who dug her keys into the sides of the man's car and carved up its leather seats.

Sadly, that song reflects not merely understandable anger but calculated revenge. For other sinned-against spouses, the response remains more inward. Some are crushed, immobilized, feeling hopeless and helpless. Others try to press on, carry out their other duties, and pursue normalcy, but fears, doubts, and questions nag them.

As we move forward we'll consider other responses. But first I want to describe a different way to respond, one expressing God's work in a sinned-against spouse. Cassie tells her story:

> If you had told me one year earlier—when my husband's affair was uncovered—that we

would be together today, I would have laughed at you. If you told me our marriage would be strong, I would have called you cruel. But that's exactly what God has brought out. All is not ideal; he is far from being a perfect husband (or me a perfect wife), and doubts and memories still invade me. But what we have learned about ourselves and about our Lord is priceless. Praise God, who really does redeem dirty things and makes them shine![2]

By God's grace, Cassie[3] and her husband experienced restoration in their marriage. The Lord used counseling and many of the biblical concepts in this book to not only help them individually but to grow and strengthen their marriage after his adultery.

Of course, Scripture doesn't guarantee marital restoration. Deanna's experience differed from Cassie's:

My husband had several affairs, and despite sincere, serious, and repeated intervention attempts by our pastors, a biblical counselor in our church, and several godly men, he refused to repent. Yet the Lord used this entire ordeal—over the course of a year or two—to show how much I had been building my life on my husband and not on Christ, my Rock and my Redeemer. So, amid the pain, my husband's sin became the occasion for me to turn toward the Lord and to find in him a kind of comfort previously unknown to me.

As Cassie's and Deanna's accounts remind us, it takes two to restore a marriage. The offender must repent, and both partners must trust and obey the Lord. That happened in Cassie's case but not in Deanna's.

As we begin our journey, we must recognize that God doesn't promise you restoration with your spouse. He only promises to be with you as a Christian—to help you know, follow, love, and enjoy him, however your spouse chooses to behave.

During my near-forty years of pastoral ministry, I have counseled various Cassies (with repentant husbands) and Deannas (with unrepentant husbands), as well as husbands of adulterous wives who did or didn't repent. But however the offending spouses acted, when the sinned-against spouses turned to God, even in small and weak steps, the Lord used this tragic thing to draw them closer to him and bring about a greater good in their life. That's my hope for you, and the hope God guarantees.

MY AUDIENCE

I am writing this book for two categories of readers. My primary audience is those who have been betrayed by their spouse. These principles can also apply to those who have been betrayed in serious dating or engagement relationships. While the focus is on sexual infidelity, the truths can relate to other forms of marital unfaithfulness as well, such as financial deceit, emotional affairs, and intimate partner violence.

The second category of readers are those who seek to love, befriend, and minister to someone who has suffered such infidelity. If you are in this second category, I thank God for you. The church of Jesus needs you. And those in the first category need you. I hope this book will make you wiser, more sensitive, and more confident to help those whose spouses have betrayed them. You are engaged in a challenging but rewarding ministry that reflects the gospel itself—God's work of reconciling spiritually adulterous people like you and me to himself. While the sin and the ensuing rift between your friend and their spouse grieves you, the prospects of God working in your friend's life and reconciling their marriage can motivate you.

If you are in category one and have been sinned against by an unfaithful spouse, you may find yourself in one of various stages. If you have just discovered the infidelity, your pain is recent and raw. If, however, you have survived the initial shock, perhaps you have begun the process of walking with the Lord in this new reality. Or maybe you are in a place where you have worked through many aspects this book will address, but you want to learn and grow more. While the flow of the book moves from crisis discovery toward growing in maturity, with the help of your pastors, counselors, and friends, you will need to discern which truths are needed most for you right now. But, in general, it's best to progress along the steps in order.

BEGIN WITH HOPE

Let's begin with biblical hope. The word *hope* means to desire a future positive outcome, something favorable we want to happen. We typically use it in casual ways: I hope the weather will be nice; I hope my business will succeed; I hope my children will follow Jesus. In such cases, the verb reflects good desires you want to see happen, but none are guaranteed. We can call this *small-h hope* in contrast to God's *capital-H Hope*—the good desires God has guaranteed.

The enticing problem of small-h hope

Luke 24:13–27 narrates a classic case of small-h hope in which two followers of Jesus are journeying home from Jerusalem after his death. Luke describes their faces as "downcast" (v. 17). Here's their summary of events:

> "He was a prophet, powerful in word and deed before God and all the people. The chief priests and our rulers handed him over to be sentenced to death, and they crucified him; but we had hoped that he was the one who was going to redeem Israel. And what is more, it is the third day since all this took place." (vv. 19–21)

Why were they sad? Because they had "hoped that he was the one who was going to redeem Israel" (v. 21). They expected a Messiah who would overthrow Rome, restore the Davidic dynasty, and exalt Israel to its proper place. But their anticipated Messiah was now dead and their earthly hopes with him. Of course, they were not entirely wrong. One day God will judge the nations, vindicate his followers, and establish Jesus as our earthly King. But their timing was wrong. As we read this story on this side of the cross, we smile at the irony in their mindset: *he was supposed to redeem us but instead he died*. They failed to grasp that Christ's death was the precise way he would redeem them. Jesus responded by rebuking their failure to believe their own Old Testament prophets and reminding them the Messiah first had to suffer (vv. 25–26). He then patiently explained the Scriptures, walked alongside them, entered their home, stayed with them, and taught them further (vv. 27–32).

We can take away a principle from this interaction between Jesus and these disciples: Never put your hope in what God has not guaranteed.

What legitimate small-h hopes must you guard against making into capital-H Hopes? First, you must not expect God to remove all your troubling feelings. Your grief, anger, fear, or whatever assorted emotions you feel are common, understandable responses to disappointed small-h hopes. Some might be godly responses, and some might not be; many are mixtures of good and bad because our emotions reflect the Spirit as well as the flesh. In time, the sinful emotions often dissipate, and new Spirit-formed emotions emerge. But you can't rid yourself of those negative feelings directly; you must allow the Lord to help you in his timing.

Second, you must not expect God to restore your marriage, nor should you make that your goal. Of course, it's the best small-h hope you can, and should, have. But you have no guarantee your spouse will repent and follow Jesus. Don't fix your hope on a goal you can't unilaterally achieve.

Third, you must not expect God to undo the consequences of your spouse's sin. You are facing hardships you neither expected nor deserved. The sooner you conceptualize the adultery and its consequences as a trial and a form of suffering, not some category outside of Scripture, the sooner you can absorb God's Word and receive his help. God doesn't promise the alleviation of suffering in this life. Sin brings consequences. It severely complicates life, whether it's the effects of sin from Adam and Eve or the current sin of your marriage partner.

God's capital-H Hope for you

So, if you can't find hope in fixing your emotional hurts, your spouse, your marriage, or in reversing the effects of their sinful choices, where do you find it? In the Bible. It offers you a better hope—God's capital-H Hope: the presence of Almighty God and all his promises now and in the days to come. The triune God—Father, Son, and Holy Spirit—promises to be with you, watch over you, and walk with you through the entire aftermath of your spouse's infidelity.

We will unpack these in the coming chapters. But for now, I encourage you to turn to God. Only he can fully understand you and guide you through this trial. I want you to be able to trust God your Father, the One who is sovereign, wise, and good in all things. He loves you more than you can fathom, proving it by sending his Son to die and be raised for you, while you were "powerless . . . ungodly . . . [a sinner and] God's enemies" (Romans 5:6–11). And this was just the start of the Father's love for you. Romans 8:32 goes further, "He who did not spare his own Son, but gave him up for us all—how will he not also, along with him, graciously give us all things?" And those things include "everything we need for a godly life through our knowledge of him who called us by his own glory and goodness" (2 Peter 1:3). The Father is with you. The Father watches over you. And the Father will be with you through the aftermath of your spouse's infidelity.

I want you to be able to trust your Lord Jesus Christ as the One who has been made like you in every way and has been tempted like you in every way (Hebrews 2:17; 4:15). He understands you. His three closest friends fell asleep on him in the garden of Gethsemane. Judas betrayed him to his murderers. Peter denied him three times. And all his disciples abandoned him, as Matthew 26:56 records, "Then all the disciples deserted him and fled." Jesus was alone when facing his worst suffering. And as our suffering, compassionate Savior, he can help you follow his model as you walk with him down the difficult path you face.

And I want you to trust the Holy Spirit—the Spirit of Christ who resides within you—to use this ordeal to make you more like Jesus each day. He enables you to believe and obey the Lord, and to cry out as an adopted son or daughter to God as your Father.[4] Furthermore, even when you face severe conflicts (Galatians 5:13–15), the Spirit empowers you to live a life marked by "love, joy, peace, forbearance, kindness, goodness, faithfulness, gentleness and self-control" (Galatians 5:22–23).

If this capital-H Hope seems too good to be true, or if the implications of following Christ seem overwhelming, be encouraged; you're in good company. Absorbing these biblical truths takes time. Remember that Jesus Christ died on the cross and rose from the dead precisely to make all these things real for you. You can take courage because he did what you can't. And so I simply extend to you the same assurance God extended to Cassie and Deanna:

> Now may the God of peace, who through the blood of the eternal covenant brought back from the dead our Lord Jesus, that great Shepherd of the sheep, equip you with everything good for doing his will, and may he work in us what is pleasing to him, through Jesus Christ, to whom be glory for ever and ever. Amen. (Hebrews 13:20–21)

Jesus is with you. He bled and died and rose for you. He will equip you. He is your great Shepherd. He is working in you. Whatever our Lord calls you to do, he will enable you to do it.

HOW TO BENEFIT FROM THIS BOOK

As you continue, I'd like to suggest three commitments that will help you.

First, read this book along with an open Bible to look up and reflect on passages and to commune prayerfully with your Lord. Ask him to reveal himself to you through his Word. Consider what the psalmist says in Psalm 119:116, "Sustain me, my God, according to your promise, and I will live." In the face of an experience that brings you through a dark valley, God's Word can bring us life. We need his life-giving Word. Amid the chaos of adultery, we need the promise of verse 165 to stabilize our soul, "Great peace have those who love your law, and nothing can make them stumble."

Assured by verses like these, you can pray, "Father, I need your help. I don't know how to handle this crisis, but I believe your Word will sustain me and stabilize me. Help me glean from your Word what I need to know and do to please you and live in light of these promises."

I also recommend you read this entire book first to understand the big picture, but then implement the steps in the order presented. As I noted earlier, you might be experiencing and handling the infidelity in differing ways than others, so certain chapters might be more timely for you than others. No book can discern that for you. To give you an overview, chapters 3, 4, and 5 take you along the path of connecting with God, discerning how he wants you to view the betrayal, and then engaging your spouse. Interacting with your spouse in chapter 5 without the truths in chapters 3 and 4 will be ineffective and counterproductive.

Second, to best benefit from this book, seek the help of your pastor(s) and two or three fellow church members, assuming you belong to a healthy, Christ-centered church that teaches the gospel and cares for its members in biblical ways. If this doesn't describe your church, find one immediately and begin attending it with a view to joining it. Consider the power and beauty of the body of Christ when we face a hardship like infidelity.

In his church, the Lord provides pastors and Christian brothers and sisters who can weep and suffer alongside us and insightfully counsel us (Proverbs 20:5; Romans 12:15; 15:14; 1 Corinthians 12:25–26). We don't need to bear these burdens alone or navigate the confusing path of handling adultery without the wise, compassionate care of others. Just as you need God's Word, you also need his people.

Inform your pastor, who can shepherd you through this, counsel you biblically, connect you to a biblical counselor in the church or community, and in many cases, reach out to your spouse. Along with counseling, share your struggle with one or two same-gender, godly, caring church members. Invite them to befriend you, walk with you, pray with you, and provide support and accountability as you follow this difficult path. If you are not sure whom to approach, ask your pastor or counselor for suggestions. I recommend that the people you choose read this book with you and use it as a guide to help you. They could even come with you to the counseling sessions to help reinforce the biblical counsel you are receiving.

For the purpose of this book, I will typically use the term "your counselors" to refer to whomever is helping you. That might include several individuals—pastors, friends, church-based counselors, and/or state-licensed counselors.

Third, be patient. Persevere in pursuing the Lord despite the pain, even if change comes slowly. Gut-wrenching trials rarely resolve quickly. Serious relational breaches resist immediate reconciliation. Consider this encouragement to press on:

> Consider it pure joy, my brothers and sisters, whenever you face trials of many kinds, because you know that the testing of your faith produces

perseverance. Let perseverance finish its work so that you may be mature and complete, not lacking anything. If any of you lacks wisdom, you should ask God, who gives generously to all without finding fault, and it will be given to you. (James 1:2–5; cf. 1:12; Romans 5:1–5)

Having counseled many couples in cases of infidelity, I assure you that by making these commitments, the Lord will use the biblical truths in this book to help you handle this crisis in ways that please him and strengthen your faith.

QUESTIONS FOR REFLECTION OR DISCUSSION

1. What uncertainties or fears do you face as you begin to read this book and apply its Christ-centered counsel?

2. Where do you find yourself struggling to gain and maintain capital-H Hope?

3. Who is your counseling team?

Chapter 2

IDENTIFYING YOUR HARDSHIPS AND TEMPTATIONS

Before we explore how to respond to your spouse's infidelity (chapters 3 and following), let's process your experience through a biblical lens.

WHAT HAPPENED TO YOU

Let me encourage you to think biblically about what happened to you. Whether your spouse's adultery was a onetime incident or an extended affair, at least three things are true.

First, you were *sinned against*. Period.

We can supply numerous synonyms: You were betrayed, cheated on, cuckolded. Your spouse hooked up with someone else. While these might be descriptively helpful, biblically viewing what happened to you begins with calling your spouse's behavior what it is—sin.

Second, your spouse's sin was not your fault. Your spouse's sins were your spouse's sins. You are not responsible for someone else's choices. The apostle James declares clearly, "Each person is tempted when they are dragged away by their own evil desire and enticed. Then, after desire has conceived, it gives birth to sin; and sin, when it is full-grown, gives birth to death" (James 1:14–15). Though you are a sinner, your sins and human limitations never justify your spouse's adultery. Nothing you did or failed to do justifies that.

Third, your spouse's sin of adultery was not like the typical sins that married couples must deal with. Your spouse violated your marital one-flesh relationship and the covenant vows made before God, the wedding witnesses, and you. Sin, of course, marks every marriage. James reminds us that "we all stumble in many ways" (James 3:2). And the apostle John says, "If we claim to be without sin, we deceive ourselves and the truth is not in us" (1 John 1:8). But this kind of sin is different. Adultery strikes at the heart of marriage. While all sin is grievous, this particular sin is more serious than other marital sins. Consider these four reasons:

1. Scripture defines the heart of marriage in Genesis 2:24: "That is why a man leaves his father and mother and is united to his wife, and they become one flesh." In marriage, we forsake all others, unite with our spouse, and form a one-flesh union for life. In marriage, God joins together what should not be broken. Any breach is serious. Moses wrote these words not only in reference to the original marriage of Adam and Eve, but also for his Israelite audience as they prepared to enter the new land. Jesus cites this same verse in Matthew 19:5

to reinforce the permanence and inseparability of marriage. The apostle Paul also quoted it in 1 Corinthians 6:16 to prohibit sexual infidelity and in Ephesians 5:31 to show the mysterious parallel between the one-flesh union of marriage and the intimate spiritual union between Christ and his church. Adultery attacks the very foundation on which God built marriage.

2. The description of marriage in Genesis 2 pictures something greater than a mere human contract or agreement (like taking a job or choosing a college), but a covenant, a sacred mutual commitment involving vows made in God's sight. Proverbs 2:16–19 and Malachi 2:13–16 explicitly call marriage a covenant. Adultery violates a covenant God himself instituted.

3. Adultery is more serious than other marital sins in that it provides one of the two exceptions Jesus and his apostles gave when forbidding divorce (Matthew 5:32; 19:9). Adultery can end a marriage.

4. Along with idolatry, adultery and its synonyms appear throughout Scripture as a common metaphor for Israel's rejection of the Lord. For example, in Ezekiel 6:9, God describes "how I have been grieved by their adulterous hearts, which have turned away from me, and by their eyes, which have lusted after their idols." James 4:4 uses this same metaphor to warn of the dangers of spiritual adultery. In one sense, God likens marital adultery with rejecting him.

Taken together, these four points underscore the gravity of this sin over other marital sins. I remind you of this because I have sometimes heard adulterous spouses try to equate their adultery with the lesser sins of the other spouse, as if to somehow excuse or minimize their adultery. While no marriage partner is sinless, infidelity rises to a different level of severity.

A tragic psalm

Psalm 55 presents a vivid image of the experience of betrayal. In it, we hear the heartbeat of a person devastated by intimate betrayal. Can you locate your own experience in this psalm? David begins in verses 1–3 by crying out to God in the face of enemy opposition to "listen to my prayer." Verses 4–11 provide further and fuller descriptions of his suffering at the hands of wicked enemies. But in verses 12–14 we learn something even more tragic about the identity of those seeking to destroy him. The leader is David's close friend:

> If an enemy were insulting me,
>   I could endure it;
> if a foe were rising against me,
>   I could hide.
> But it is you, a man like myself,
>   my companion, my close friend,
> with whom I once enjoyed sweet fellowship
>   at the house of God,
> as we walked about
>   among the worshipers.

The parallels with marital betrayal are plain. The person is "like myself," reminding us of Adam's "bone of my bones" response to seeing Eve and of their one-flesh relationship (Genesis 2:23–24). He is David's "companion" and "close friend," terms reminiscent of the marriage "partner" synonyms in Proverbs 2:17 and

Malachi 2:14—passages also envisioning adultery. He and David once "enjoyed sweet fellowship" as fellow worshipers in the temple, similar to you and your spouse going to church together. It's one thing to be betrayed by an enemy; it's another to be betrayed by your close friend, especially if that close friend is your marriage partner, your other half.

So, what happened to you? From God's perspective, here's the bottom line: You were sinned against in an extremely hurtful way by your God-given covenantal partner. Yet God listens to you, understands your suffering, and invites you to "cast your cares" on him because "he will sustain you" and "will never let the righteous be shaken" (Psalm 55:22).

WHAT'S HAPPENING IN YOU

I can't pretend to know what you are experiencing, and I don't want to presume your struggle is like those I have counseled. There are many and varied thoughts and feelings you might be experiencing. Each seems quite understandable given the crisis you have faced. Which of the following describe you?[1]

☐ You might feel *confused, ignorant, or in the dark.* "I thought I knew my spouse, but now it's clear that I don't." "How did this all happen? I'm clueless." Depending on the nature of his or her sin and how and when it was discovered or voluntarily disclosed, there are dozens of details you lack, and you'd like to know: How did they meet? When did it happen? Where? How many times? For how long? Is it really over? Who knows about it? Is he or she repentant? Your questions, understandably, might be endless.

☐ You might feel *grief, sadness, or despair.* "I'll never get over this. My life is over." As the late Queen Elizabeth II famously put it, "Grief is the price we pay for love." Even if your marriage was not perfect, you nevertheless have lost someone you loved and valued. These thoughts and feelings might even lead to the deep, debilitating sadness of hopelessness or depression.

☐ You might feel *angry, and that anger can manifest itself in many different revealed or concealed forms.* Angry at whom? Your spouse: "I hate my spouse for what he or she did." Or the adulterous partner: "I despise the person my partner slept with." Or your spouse's friends or relatives that kept this sin hidden: "I can't believe they didn't tell me or force my spouse to confess." Or God: "I've served God faithfully, and this is how he rewards me?"

☐ You might feel *jealous*: "I can't believe he picked her over me." "What did she see in him?" Or more subtle forms of jealousy might arise—envying others with happy marriages and faithful spouses.

☐ You might feel *worried, anxious, or fearful*. Part of this involves uncertainty: "What's going to happen next?" Many unknowns certainly exist. The consequences of your spouse's betrayal might have already had a harmful effect on your children, your lifestyle, and your finances.

☐ You might feel *regret or guilt*. "I know I've failed as a wife; I drove him into her arms." "If only I had been a better husband, she wouldn't have cheated."

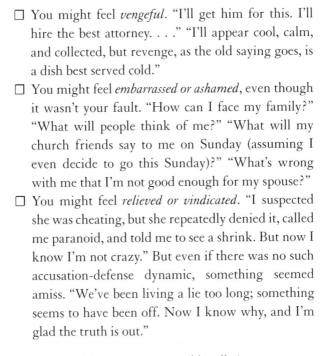

☐ You might feel *vengeful*. "I'll get him for this. I'll hire the best attorney. . . ." "I'll appear cool, calm, and collected, but revenge, as the old saying goes, is a dish best served cold."

☐ You might feel *embarrassed or ashamed*, even though it wasn't your fault. "How can I face my family?" "What will people think of me?" "What will my church friends say to me on Sunday (assuming I even decide to go this Sunday)?" "What's wrong with me that I'm not good enough for my spouse?"

☐ You might feel *relieved or vindicated*. "I suspected she was cheating, but she repeatedly denied it, called me paranoid, and told me to see a shrink. But now I know I'm not crazy." But even if there was no such accusation-defense dynamic, something seemed amiss. "We've been living a lie too long; something seems to have been off. Now I know why, and I'm glad the truth is out."

Or consider one more possible, albeit uncommon, response indicating a different and deeper problem.

☐ You might feel *happy or free*. Maybe infidelity is the latest display of other serious marital sins, so you are glad you can finally ask your spouse to leave. Or maybe you have your eyes on someone else and have no biblical way out of your marriage, but your spouse's infidelity has opened a door of escape.

This list reminds us that our hearts are continually active, and they can respond in an endless variety of ways. Maybe you can think of others. Or perhaps your experience is a mosaic of all those listed above.

Knowing how *your* heart is responding to *your* spouse's betrayal is key to discovering how you will draw near to the Lord. It will enable you to find out what help you specifically need. It will also help you avoid several common pitfalls, to which we now turn.

PAY ATTENTION TO YOUR OWN RESPONSES

While we could address each of the heart responses in the previous list, I want to alert you to seven attitudes and actions that are particularly corrosive to your own soul and can hinder any effort to rebuild your marriage.

1. *Beware of anger, bitterness, or vengeance that will hinder your relationship with the Lord and render you unwilling to work on reconciling with your spouse.* While being betrayed might justify some form of righteous anger, the temptation toward sinful anger is close at hand. Don't automatically assume your anger is Christlike.[2]

2. *Beware of making rash decisions.* Running to an attorney, keeping your children from seeing their other parent, draining your joint accounts or freezing your spouse's access, or leaving or asking your spouse to leave are serious choices that you must not make without godly counsel.

3. *Beware of gossip and prematurely or unnecessarily involving others.* Aside from seeking godly counsel from your counselor(s) and the prayer and accountability support of a few godly brothers or sisters, it's best to limit your conversations. Especially avoid social media comments. Even telling your parents or family

members might be unwise apart from godly counsel. While your heart is tender and you are tempted to speak out, wisdom must prevail.

4. *Beware of competing counsel.* The sources of unwise counsel can vary: well-meaning but unwise friends or relatives, therapists who don't counsel biblically, and books, articles, and blog posts that look attractive but lack scriptural wisdom.

5. *Beware of despair and hopelessness, attitudes that see no reason to make any effort to reconcile with your spouse.* "How can we ever get beyond this?" "How will I be able to trust him?" The breadth of this problem and your own limitations can overwhelm you and make it difficult to entrust to the Lord these legitimate concerns.

6. *Beware of cynicism, the attitude that assumes you or your spouse will never change* (e.g., "I'll never get over this," or "He'll never repent."). Such predictions entirely dismiss the presence and work of the Holy Spirit.

7. *Beware of the confused form of guilt that comes when we take responsibility for our spouse's sins.* When we place ourselves under some law that isn't God's law and then violate our wrongly informed conscience, we will feel guilty. For example, if you wrongly believe "I am responsible to keep my spouse faithful," or "I must be everything my spouse demands me to be," then you will be filled with guilt when your spouse commits adultery.[3] Rejecting such unbiblical laws will liberate you.

My Christian brother or sister, amid all your varied responses and the temptations that your spouse's infidelity has caused, know that your Redeemer understands these struggles and has given you his Holy Spirit to help. With all these temptations, cry out to God's Spirit to produce in you his fruit, especially the fruit of self-control amid the unwanted provocations your spouse's sin has brought into your life. Our Lord has given you pastors and church members to come alongside you to comfort, exhort, and protect you. And he has given you his Word, with the sweet and stabilizing promise of Psalm 119:165, "Great peace have those who love your law, and nothing can make them stumble." Let him strengthen your soul by his Word, his church, and his Spirit.

QUESTIONS FOR REFLECTION OR DISCUSSION

1. While recognizing adultery as more serious than other marital sins can help explain the depth of your hurt and betrayal, it can also tempt you toward rage and bitterness. How well are you grasping the former while resisting the latter?

2. What emotions do you most often feel in response to the infidelity? Are you describing them to your counseling support team?

3. Which of the seven "bewares" tempt you? How well are you resisting those temptations?

Chapter 3

DRAWING NEAR TO YOUR GRACIOUS, COMPASSIONATE GOD

How should you handle the sobering discovery that your spouse has been unfaithful? How would God want you to think about it and respond to it? In this and the next three chapters, we will present ten steps to take. Let's begin with your relationship with God.

As you proceed, remember the truths we have already considered. The triune God—Father, Son, and Holy Spirit—is with you and for you. While you might experience fluctuating emotions and confused thoughts, his Word can provide peace, hope, and direction. You have been betrayed in a serious way by your covenant partner, and learning to handle it is a process that takes time and requires patience. Keep these realities in mind as you and your Lord move forward. Expect that you will need to prayerfully review them often.

STEP 1: BELIEVE GOD IS POWERFULLY PRESENT TO HELP YOU

In its many passages describing crises, Scripture frequently weaves together two of God's attributes: his presence and his power. Psalm 46:1–3 provides a dramatic example:

> God is our refuge and strength,
> an ever-present help in trouble.
> Therefore we will not fear, though the earth give
> way
> and the mountains fall into the heart of the sea,
> though its waters roar and foam
> and the mountains quake with their
> surging.

The devastating earthquake scene described in this psalm resonated with Amy after she discovered her husband of eight years had committed adultery with one of their mutual friends. "It shook my whole world. Every support was crashing in around me." Yet God's power—he's "our refuge and strength"—and "ever-present help" stabilized her soul and kept her from fear. It gave her hope that even though she felt powerless and out of control, God was present and moving in her life. Psalm 46:5 continues this assurance, referring to Israel's holy city, Jerusalem, "God is within her, she will not fall; God will help her at break of day," the time when ancient battles began. The twin themes then repeat in the psalm's refrain, "The LORD Almighty is with us; the God of Jacob is our fortress" (vv. 7, 11). In her moments of doubt, these truths helped assure

Amy that God would indeed hold on to her soul and empower her to handle her earthquake God's way.

God's presence and power reappear in 2 Timothy 4:16–17. The apostle Paul recalled a judicial trial he underwent. While Bible scholars differ over what specific incident Paul refers to, perhaps you can identify with his feeling of isolation:

> At my first defense, no one came to my support, but everyone deserted me. May it not be held against them. But the Lord stood at my side and gave me strength, so that through me the message might be fully proclaimed and all the Gentiles might hear it. And I was delivered from the lion's mouth.

Paul felt alone, deserted by his friends. In the preceding verses (vv. 9–15), he explains how that happened—one friend abandoned his faith, and others were deployed elsewhere in kingdom ministry. You and Paul were both abandoned. You can resonate with Paul's feelings.

But notice a second point, signaled by the tiny word, "but": "But the Lord stood at my side and gave me strength." By faith Paul envisioned Jesus with him, not physically but by his Spirit, in keeping with Jesus's promises to his disciples to be with them and to send his Spirit to help them (Matthew 28:20; John 14:16–18, 25–26).

"Knowing I truly belong to Jesus didn't bring Eric back," Amy noted, "but it did allow me to face my fears with confidence that Jesus would help me."

My brother or sister in Christ, God has not abandoned you just because your spouse did. God is with you amid your marital crisis. He is ever-present, always available, on call. He is your refuge, strength, and fortress. He stands by your side. Begin your path by striving to believe this.

STEP 2: CRY OUT TO GOD FOR HELP

In light of God's assurance of his presence and power, he invites you to cry out to him, right now, as you are. In chapter 2, we learned from Psalm 55 about David being betrayed by an intimate friend, "a man like myself, my companion, my close friend" (v. 13). How does he handle it? David cries out to God in prayer, "As for me, I call to God, and the Lord saves me. Evening, morning and noon I cry out in distress, and he hears my voice" (vv. 16–17). Notice the frequency of his outcries—morning, noon, and night. God does not limit your prayer time to a morning devotional segment, a session with your counselor, or a congregational worship service. You can come to him anytime and all the time.

Several Bible passages provide a image for prayer—to "pour out" your heart to God. In Psalm 62, while himself facing assault from enemies, David invites his readers in verse 8 to:

> Trust in him at all times, you people;
>> pour out your hearts to him,
>> for God is our refuge.

God's promises provide the ground for such confident prayer. In 1 Samuel 1:13–15, Hannah grieves her infertility, a major source of shame in her culture. While her prayers are inaudible, her moving lips prompt Eli the priest to (wrongly) accuse her of being drunk. Her response? "'Not so, my lord,' Hannah replied, 'I am a woman who is deeply troubled. I have not been drinking wine or beer; I was pouring out my soul to the LORD'" (v. 15). Her deep grief gave expression to an intense, visible outpouring in prayer to the Lord.

In Psalm 42, the psalmist longs to return from exile to be with God's people again. Amid his downcast state, he opens up his heart, "These things I remember as I pour out my soul: how I used to go to the house of God under the protection of the Mighty One" (v. 4). He pours out his sadness to God.

This verb translated "pour out" suggests full, uninhibited expression. It pictures an honest, emotive form of prayer—unrestrained, unreserved, and unrestricted engagement with God. Whether the experience of your spouse's betrayal feels like Hannah's grief, the Psalm 42 psalmist's despair, or David under attack in Psalm 62, your Father invites you to pour out your heart to him in whole-souled, spontaneous, impassioned prayer. His heart desires you to come to him with your sorrow. Don't hold back.

Practically, if you haven't done so, I recommend you begin a prayer journal in which you write down and voice your heartfelt prayers to the Lord. Do so while reflecting on passages like those above, as well as other passages that picture God's character and God's people lamenting before him. Or, you might find hymn lyrics that give voice to your experience of suffering. Hymns like "Be Still, My Soul," "Whate'er My God

Ordains Is Right," and "He Will Hold Me Fast" can reinforce what's true about your Lord amid your pain.

Will God hear you?

It's one thing to heed God's invitation to pour out your soul to him. It's another to know he will hear you. Again we turn to Scripture and some of the many verses in Psalms that assure us God hears the cries of his suffering people. We saw in Psalm 55:17 David's assurance in the midst of his distress that the Lord "hears my voice." Psalm 10 recounts the treacherous actions of those who wickedly oppress the helpless. How does the psalm resolve?

> You, Lord, hear the desire of the afflicted;
>> you encourage them, and you listen to their cry,
> defending the fatherless and the oppressed.
>> (10:17–18a)

What does the Lord do for those who cry out to him? He hears them, encourages them, listens to them, and defends them. Crying out to him is not in vain. He hears. In Psalm 34, a psalm describing David's suffering as he fled from Saul who sought to kill him, we read multiple assurances of God the listener to his distressed believers:

- "I sought the Lord, and he answered me; he delivered me from all my fears. . . . This poor man called, and the Lord heard him; he saved him out of all his troubles" (34:4, 6).

- "The eyes of the LORD are on the righteous, and his ears are attentive to their cry. . . . The righteous cry out, and the LORD hears them; he delivers them from all their troubles" (34:15, 17).

When you seek him in prayer, the Lord answers, delivers, hears, saves, and attends to your cry.

As you spend time in the Psalms, you'll hear more of these assurances (e.g., 22:24; 40:1; 86:6–7; 116:1–2; 138). Use these truths as a balm for your soul. Talk to God about your betrayal. Breathe your sorrows to him. He invites you to come to him in prayer and to pour out your heart to him.

STEP 3: RECOGNIZE YOUR CORE IDENTITY AS GOD'S SON OR DAUGHTER, NOT YOUR SPOUSE'S HUSBAND OR WIFE

Your spouse's adultery will devastate you to the same extent that he or she has functioned as your primary relationship in life. Their infidelity will crush you to the same extent that your status as a married person has primarily defined you.

This was Lisa's experience: "I fell apart when I found out what Tim had done. The bottom of my life suddenly dropped out, and I was free-falling into the darkness." Max put it more starkly: "Sara was my life. And now my life is over."[1] For Lisa, she now has no foundation for living. For Max, his life is now over. Of course, Lisa and Max might not mean what they say literally, but the metaphors carry meaning—sometimes more meaning than they realize. The flood of thoughts and feelings that come after betrayal often leaves spouses disoriented. The pain is real. The suffering is real. And yet, in the midst of the fog, they can begin to believe things that seem true, but are based in false beliefs. Embracing these false notions will only enslave you and intensify your suffering.

Instead, a growing grasp of the Bible liberates. But how? How can we grow in an understanding of where our true identity lies in the face of rejection? Let's consider several passages that contrast the ultimate dependency on God vs. other humans.

David's perspective

In Psalm 27:10, David states this contrast concisely, "Though my father and mother forsake me, the LORD will receive me." He contrasts the hardship of being "forsaken" by his parents with being "received" by the Lord. In the chart below we see how these two realities exist side by side: the Seen Reality (R #1) we see with our earthly eyes and the Unseen Reality (R #2) we see only through the eyes of faith.

The Two-Reality Rejection-Reception Chart

	Seen Reality (R #1)	Unseen Reality (R #2)
Psalm 27:10	Parents forsake me	The LORD will receive me.

The verb *forsake* suggests a strong break, a sharp turning away, and a clear abandonment. David didn't deny it or seek to get rid of the memories. Instead, the LORD's loving presence—his R #2 reception—controlled and consumed David, enabling him to live for his Lord and find comfort and strength despite the R #1 rejection.

The verb *receive* denotes a loving, caring acceptance. Notice also the uppercase "Lord"—Yahweh, the personal name of Israel's covenant-keeping God. The God who receives David is no abstract, impersonal deity but the faithful, merciful "I am" Redeemer of Israel.

How might this passage practically help you as you process your spouse's betrayal? Here are four action steps:

1. Read Psalm 27—all fourteen verses—twice a day this week.
2. Memorize verse 10 as it's written but substitute "my husband" or "my wife" for "my father and mother" in your prayers and reflections on the text.
3. Start a prayer journal in which you talk to God about your struggles, seek his help, and thank him for the progress you see.
4. As you read Psalm 27, record in your prayer journal what the psalm teaches you about the Lord—his attributes, actions, and promises. The better you know him, the better you will manage your spouse's adultery.

Further examples of rejection

We could add more rows to our chart above by reflecting on the accounts of Hagar in Genesis 16:1–16; Paul in 2 Timothy 4:9–18 (in Step 1 above); Joseph in Genesis 37–50 (in Step 5 below); and Jesus in John 16:32. Meditating on these passages and journaling prayers about them will comfort your soul and assure you of God's faithful love for you. He is for you even if your spouse was not.

The Two-Reality Rejection-Reception Chart

	Seen Reality (R #1)	Unseen Reality (R #2)
David in Psalm 27:10	Parents forsake me	The LORD will receive me.
Hagar in Genesis 16:1–16	Abram and Sarai mistreat her	The angel of the LORD finds, speaks to, hears, sees her.
Paul in 2 Timothy 4:9–18	Deserted during court trial	The Lord stood by my side and gave me strength.
Joseph in Genesis 37, 39–50	Various forms of betrayal	The LORD was with Joseph and blessed Joseph.
John 16:32	Disciples (closest earthly friends) leave me all alone.	My Father is with me, therefore, I am not alone.

Let's consider the John 16 passage. It vividly captures the importance of a God-defined identity as God's son or daughter amid betrayal. On the eve of his crucifixion, Jesus teaches many things to his disciples and then issues an ominous prediction in 16:32, "A time is coming and in fact has come when you will be scattered, each to your own home. You will leave me all alone. Yet I am not alone, for my Father is with me."

The Gospel narratives confirmed this reality; shortly afterward, the disciples all abandon Jesus. Yet this did not devastate our Lord. Instead, he declares, "Yet I am not alone." How can a person be "not alone" when all his closest earthly friends abandon him? Because Someone else is present with him—Someone whose presence trumps, outweighs, and overrides the absence of those friends: "for my Father is with me."

The presence of his Father comforted Jesus when everyone else left him. In the same way, his Father's presence as *your* Father can comfort you as his son or daughter in the aftermath of your partner's infidelity. Since you belong to Jesus, his Father is your Father, and his Father's love for him extends to you!

I close this chapter with my response to an email I received between my counseling sessions with Kathy, whose husband, Edward, had been adulterous. They were separated, and he teetered on recommitting to their marriage. In her email she grieved her various losses. Here's my response:

Kathy,

What you shared makes sense to me, and I can feel the frustration of wanting Edward to commit to you and to your marriage. All your emotions of sadness, frustration, anger, despair, and weariness make sense. I'd be surprised if they were absent.

But amid this confusion, as we began to discuss in our last meeting, I'd like to help you gain a bigger vision, the vision of what it means—practically and meaningfully—to find a deeper measure of joy, peace, and contentment in Jesus so that your desire for Edward is not vanquished or neutered but placed in a bigger context. To the extent that we make our spouse our life, to that extent, when that person fails us or pulls away from us, our life will obviously and of course, by definition, be over, on hold, and miserable.

And to that extent you have yielded your joy, peace, and contentment into Edward's control. But to the extent Jesus and his forgiveness, love, power, and presence control your heart, to that extent you will have life, joy, peace, and contentment, even if Edward doesn't love you the way we or even God thinks he should.

Trust me, Kathy, this is not pie-in-the-sky but available to you in Jesus, and we can help you. Consider passages like Psalm 27:10 (subbing "my husband" for "my mother and father"); 73:23–28; Luke 10:20; 10:38–42; 12:32; John 16:32; and Philippians 4:11–13 in the coming days. We can discuss this in our next session.

QUESTIONS FOR REFLECTION OR DISCUSSION

1. This chapter covered three biblical truths: God's powerful presence, his call to pray and his assurance he will hear you, and your core identity as God's son or daughter. How well are these truths comforting and encouraging you?

2. What problems do you experience when you try to pray? Have you shared these with your counselor(s)?

3. What other identities compete with God's declaration of your daughterhood or sonship? Husband or wife? Son or daughter? Mom or dad of your children? How might that affect you in light of the adultery?

Chapter 4

HUMBLY RESPONDING
TO GOD

In this chapter we consider three more steps—how you should respond to God through the crisis.

STEP 4: SEEK TO OBEY AND PLEASE GOD, NO MATTER WHAT

Your spouse's betrayal brings you to a crossroads. Our first three steps connected you more deeply to God, but now you have a choice to make. In response to God's presence and promises, will you seek to trust, love, and obey him—no matter what happens?

In Joshua 1, after Moses died, the Lord called Joshua to lead the Israelites into the new land the Lord had promised them. You, of course, are not Joshua. God didn't call you to lead your country or defeat pagan nations. But, like Joshua and all the Israelites, you are called to follow the Lord, to enter a new life circumstance you did not choose, and to navigate a host of unknown trials and temptations. What Joshua, you, and every son or daughter of God needs is God's Word to encourage and direct us. Here's what God called Joshua to do:

> "Be strong and very courageous. Be careful to obey all the law my servant Moses gave you; do not turn from it to the right or to the left, that you may be successful wherever you go. Keep this Book of the Law always on your lips; meditate on it day and night, so that you may be careful to do everything written in it. Then you will be prosperous and successful. Have I not commanded you? Be strong and courageous. Do not be afraid; do not be discouraged, for the Lord your God will be with you wherever you go." (Joshua 1:7–9)

We can draw three applications for you:

1. You need strength and courage in the new situation you face. God promises to give you that and to provide what you need. While you are not Joshua, the same directives and promises were given to all God's people in Deuteronomy 31:6,12; 32:46.

2. You can be confident knowing that God will successfully accomplish what he wills for you. While in Joshua's case that meant military victory, as we saw in chapter 1 above, we don't know circumstantially what that will entail for you—your spouse repenting or not, the marriage being restored or not, how others will respond, etc. But the success you can expect—your

capital-H Hope—is growing Christlikeness, bearing the fruit of God's Spirit, and shining Christ's light to those around you. In this you will find the fullness of joy you deeply desire.

3. You can enjoy these blessings by carefully knowing and obeying God's Word. Note his words: "be careful," "all the law," not turning from it "to the right or to the left," "always on your lips," meditating on it "day and night," to do "everything" written in God's Law. The rest of the book of Joshua records instances where Israel's specific obedience or disobedience to God's law brought success or failure.

View your Bible as the way to know God's will for your life and commit yourself completely to obeying everything it teaches, whatever happens. The prospect of knowing and doing what Scripture teaches might overwhelm you right now, especially if the betrayal is recent and raw, and if your thoughts and emotions seem chaotic. Be patient; absorbing God's Word is a process. Here are three ways to help you take in the Bible: (1) Your private Bible reading, including prayerfully reviewing the passages in this book. (2) The regular preaching and teaching of God's Word in your corporate church gatherings. Taking notes and capturing key takeaways from your pastor's sermons can help. (3) The biblically based, private counseling that your pastor(s) and/or biblical counseling team provide for you, tailored to your specific situation. As you seek to know and do what God wants, let your support team guide you and provide encouragement and accountability.

STEP 5: EMBRACE GOD'S SOVEREIGN, WISE, LOVING PURPOSES IN YOUR SUFFERING

Many sufferers who believe in God understandably ask this question: "How can a sovereign, all-powerful God who claims to be good allow this particular form of suffering into my life?" If you have asked this—and I assume you have—you are not alone. It's the age-old problem God's people have wrestled with for millennia. This mega-question lies beneath every Bible account of human suffering caused by the sins of others.

For you, this question might vex, perplex, or trouble you in many ways, not merely as an intellectual puzzle but as a hindrance in your relationship with God. Carlos struggled with this: "I sought the Lord before I married Gwenn. I prayed a lot, pursued premarital counseling, and received confirmation from my friends and her friends that she was a godly woman. I've sought to love her, serve her, and provide for her. And then she cheated on me. I know Gwenn's sin is Gwenn's sin. But why did God let this happen to me? I've been a faithful husband. Couldn't God have stopped it somehow?"

While we must admit a certain level of mystery in our understanding of this question, we must hold tenaciously to a pair of truths in Scripture: *God is absolutely sovereign over everything, and people are morally responsible for their actions before him.*[1] Scripture consistently teaches both and treats them together as mutually compatible. While even the greatest theological minds wrestle with these matters, seeking to cling to both strands of biblical truth will increasingly stabilize your soul.

God's sovereignty over every event

Scripture repeatedly declares God's absolute sovereignty over every event. Amid our philosophical debates about the free will of mankind, Psalm 115:3 towers above those speculations by declaring the ultimate free will of God, "Our God is in heaven; he does whatever pleases him." In Daniel 4, King Nebuchadnezzar learned this truth the hard way. Amid his arrogant opposition to God, God humbled him, leading the king to proclaim

> All the peoples of the earth
>   are regarded as nothing.
> He does as he pleases
>   with the powers of heaven
>   and the peoples of the earth.
> No one can hold back his hand
>   or say to him: "What have you done?"
>   (Daniel 4:35)

God does "as he pleases" in heaven and on earth, and no one can stop him or justly object to his ways. The apostle Paul practically develops this truth in Acts 17:26–28, where he states that sovereignty extends to the details of our lives, including where we were born, where and how long we live, and what happens to us. In short, there is no corner of your life beyond God's loving care and wise control.

God is sovereign over suffering

But what about evil done to us, including various forms of unjust mistreatment and betrayal? Is

God sovereign over that? Let's consider a few biblical examples.

Genesis 37

Joseph's brothers sinned against him in severe ways. They hated him, mocked him, sought to kill him, and later sold him into slavery. Years later, when Joseph was in a position to exact revenge, he instead responded with gracious restraint and a deep grasp of God's sovereign purposes behind their evil acts, "Don't be afraid. Am I in the place of God? You intended to harm me, but God intended it for good to accomplish what is now being done, the saving of many lives" (Genesis 50:19–20). Yet, alongside his grasp of God's sovereignty, Joseph also wept upon seeing his brothers (42:24; 45:1–2). He was also strengthened by God's presence at key points in his journey (e.g., 39:2, 20–21; 45:5–8).

2 Samuel 16:5–14

King David recognized God's sovereign hand at work in God allowing Shimei, a relative of Saul and a supporter of David's rebel son Absalom, to pelt David and his men with stones and curse David. When David's men wanted to defend David and cut off Shimei's head, David replied, "Leave him alone; let him curse, for the LORD has told him to. It may be that the LORD will look upon my misery and restore to me his covenant blessing instead of his curse today" (vv. 11b–12).

Job 1–2

Job suffered severe losses—his wealth, all ten of his children, and his health, with boils from head to toe.

The direct agents were natural disasters, neighboring invaders, and Satan himself. Yet a careful study reveals that everyone in the storyline understood all these tragedies ultimately came from the sovereign, wise, and good hand of the Lord who had purposes beyond Job's understanding. God, not Satan, mentioned Job's name to Satan and gave Satan permission to bring suffering (1:8, 12; 2:3, 6). Satan knew that he had no power to harm Job unless God allowed him (1:10–12; 2:5–6); Satan and God are not equal powers. The messenger in 1:16 understood that the fire that fell was "the fire of God." Job himself understood that God was behind Job's suffering (1:21–22; 2:10), as did his wife (2:9). Job's perspective was stunningly accurate,

> "Naked I came from my mother's womb,
>   and naked I will depart.
> The LORD gave and the LORD has taken away;
>   may the name of the LORD be praised."
>   (Job 1:21)

Even the writer underscores God's sovereignty. In his forty-two chapter book, his last reference to Satan occurs in 2:7. The writer continues with forty more chapters addressing why God allowed Job's tragic losses, with no mention of Satan's involvement. The story ends in Job 42 in two ways: Job repents, not of any sinful behavior, but of demanding that God explain why he did what he did. And God then restores Job and doubles the blessings he receives.

As you reflect on these biblical accounts, in light of your marital betrayal, how are you responding? These passages can be difficult to process during this season of personal suffering. But remember that growth in grace and godliness takes time. It's a process. The same Lord who helped Joseph, David, and Job will help you as you walk with him and as you pray, immerse yourself in his Word, and seek godly counsel and support in your church.

We could survey many more examples of God's absolute sovereignty that lies behind even the sins of others.[2] But if you're struggling with this idea, know you're not alone. The Lord is with you. He knows what deep betrayal is like because he experienced it himself. Let's consider one more example, in some ways the most striking. In the apostle Peter's Acts 2 sermon to his fellow Israelites on the day of Pentecost, notice how he describes the death of Jesus the Messiah: "This man was handed over to you by God's deliberate plan and foreknowledge; and you, with the help of wicked men, put him to death by nailing him to the cross. But God raised him from the dead" (Acts 2:23–24). God planned what wicked men accomplished: the death of his Son, Jesus Christ. Jesus suffered the ultimate betrayal, yet it was part of God's sovereign plan.

What can you learn about your spouse's betrayal from these passages? It doesn't mean your spouse isn't 100 percent responsible for the infidelity or that God somehow made your partner sin (James 1:13–15). It doesn't mean God delighted in what happened to you or did not weep over your suffering. It does mean, however, that he wasn't asleep when your spouse chose infidelity. It does mean that in some inexplicable way, beyond our comprehension and without compromising his holiness, justice, and goodness, our sovereign, wise, and loving God decreed what happened. The alternative is worse—an impotent God who can only respond to the choices of his creatures and can't bring about the good purposes he sovereignly designs. God is always good in his sovereignty, even when we can't understand his perfect, infinite ways.

God's sovereign purposes in being sinned against

While the mysteries of God's sovereignty and human responsibility befuddle the brightest minds, we can find comfort in knowing God has good purposes for his people amid our suffering. After describing the groaning of God's fallen creation, including in us, Paul concludes in Romans 8:28, "And we know that in all things God works for the good of those who love him, who have been called according to his purpose." What is the good that God wants for us? Verse 29 continues, "For those God foreknew he also predestined to be conformed to the image of his Son, that he might be the firstborn among many brothers and sisters." God's goal is to make you increasingly like Jesus, his Son, which is your ultimate good. God is making you into something new through this experience. His work is purposeful and always motivated by his goodness and love. He is making you like Jesus.

And this purpose remains sure no matter how your spouse or anyone else behaves, or whether your marriage gets restored, worsens, or ends. And one day that will be revealed in your final glorification (v. 30).

But how, exactly, does God use trials to bring about greater Christlikeness? Consider seven ways God uses hardships—including relational betrayal—to make us more like Jesus.[3]

1. *God lovingly uses your hardships to enhance your relationship with him.* Suffering Christians tend to become more God-conscious and turn to him. As we saw in chapter 3, God promises to be with you and to empower you in special ways as you face your trial. The fact that you are reading this book and seeking biblical help from your church means the Lord is active in your life, seeking to conform you into Christ's image.

So, could it be that our sovereign, wise, and loving God allowed this betrayal to enter your life to make you more like Jesus?

2. *God lovingly uses your hardships to help you experience Christ's sufferings.* Our sufferings are light compared to those of our Suffering Savior. He understands betrayal. His own brothers rejected his claims and didn't believe him. The leader of his apostles pledged outspoken allegiance but three times denied even knowing Jesus. His closest friends, the twelve apostles, all fled from him at the cross. One of them betrayed him. Jesus can understand your sorrow over your spouse's betrayal. He's been there.

So, could it be that God allowed this betrayal so you could experience something of the fellowship of Christ's sufferings?

3. *God lovingly uses your hardships to expose your remaining sin.* God uses trials to boil away dross in us,

including our blind-spot sins. Sondra was a Christian wife abandoned by a man who chose another woman and a daily six-pack over Sondra and her God. Sitting with my wife and me on our back patio, she shared a remarkable insight: "I didn't see it then. But I see it now. I had made Don the center of my life. God in his sovereign love allowed my foundation to be torn away so that I might learn to make the Lord the center of my life." Only the Christian pursuing Jesus can see God's redeeming purpose behind his allowance of this suffering in Sondra's life.[4]

In this situation, the abandonment revealed Sondra's mixed-heart allegiances. Though she professed Christ as Lord, in reality, she looked to her husband for fulfillment. And if he didn't give her what she craved and demanded, she was devastated. Here's the principle: If I *want* you to treat me faithfully but you don't, I'll be disappointed. But if I *need* (or crave or demand) you to treat me faithfully but you don't, I'll be devastated. The difference is not about you but about me. My heart before the Lord is the variable in whether I am disappointed, hurt, or saddened or I am devastated, crushed, or enraged.

So, could it be that God allowed this betrayal to lead you to godly self-examination, repentance, and renewed devotion to Jesus?

4. *God lovingly uses your hardships to engage you in the body of Christ.* Suffering can draw us closer to other church members. In your case, if you have followed the counsel in this book, you have already connected with several church leaders and members. God wants you to

allow the body of Christ to minister to you and for you to seek to serve the body as well.

So, could it be that God allowed this betrayal to connect you more tightly to Christ's body and thus to his care?

5. *God lovingly uses your hardships to exhibit Christ's work in you.* Your trial gives you a unique opportunity to reflect Jesus to others. As you respond to the infidelity and walk forward toward (hopeful) reconciliation or (possible) divorce, your children, friends, and family members will be watching how a Christian handles being cheated on and if it's any different from the way unbelievers respond.

So, could it be that God allowed this betrayal to let you shine the light of Christ to others and show them the difference Jesus makes amid hardships?

6. *God lovingly uses your hardships to equip you for wiser, more compassionate ministry.* God comforts us in our suffering so we can comfort others. You are not the first and you won't be the last believer in your church or your community to suffer a spouse's infidelity. I think of several people whose "compassion-quotient" rose as the Lord helped them handle their spouse's affair. Some have received biblical counseling training and now minister to others who face betrayal.

So, could it be that God allowed this betrayal to make you an effective instrument to minister to others who suffer?

7. *God lovingly uses your hardships to elevate your longing for Christ's return.* Earthly hardships create a proper dissatisfaction with this fallen world and a

longing for the new heaven and earth and all the eternal blessings God promises. I don't know if your spouse will repent and seek to reconcile your marriage. If he or she does not, then know that you have something better awaiting you—the marriage supper of the Lamb. But even if your spouse does repent, then know that you still have something better awaiting you, the marriage supper of the Lamb! In other words, all our earthly marriages will one day end (Luke 20:34–39). They are but shadows and foretastes of something more glorious to come.

So, could it be that God allowed this betrayal to move you to look forward to your eternal union with Christ in the new heaven and new earth?

These seven dynamics summarize the principal ways Scripture describes God's good purposes for our suffering. Whether you realize it or not, the God who loves you and gave his Son for you is using your trial for God's glory and your good. Romans 8:28–30, referenced above, continues in verses 31–32, "What, then, shall we say in response to these things? If God is for us, who can be against us? He who did not spare his own Son, but gave him up for us all—how will he not also, along with him, graciously give us all things?"

Brother or sister, God uses the "all things" of your suffering (v. 28), including your husband or wife's infidelity, to make you like Christ (vv. 29–30). And he guarantees to give you the "all things" of his grace (v. 32)—every provision you need—a guarantee secured for you by Christ's death and resurrection. At every point, now and forever, God is *for* you (v. 31).

QUESTIONS FOR REFLECTION
OR DISCUSSION

1. How is a recognition of God's sovereignty over
    your life, including your spouse's unfaithfulness,
    affecting you? What thoughts and emotions does it
    prompt? Be sure to talk to God and your counselors
    about these.

2. Of the seven ways God uses hardships to make you
    more like Jesus, which one (or more) might he be
    using at this point in your life?

Chapter 5

GOD'S WAY TO VIEW
AND TREAT YOUR SPOUSE

Until now we have said nothing directly about how to speak to your spouse. That's been intentional. My priority has been for you to connect with God, to view the trial through his lens, and to have your heart right before him. In this chapter, we now consider how you should look at and engage with your spouse who has betrayed you.[1]

STEP 6: CULTIVATE A HEART OF MERCY AND ATTITUDINAL FORGIVENESS

Given the seriousness of the sin of infidelity, you cannot ignore, overlook, cover over, or simply forget it. Your spouse or others might request that, but God calls you instead to forgive offenders. In examining the Bible's teaching on forgiveness, it's helpful to distinguish two levels.[2] We might call the first level attitudinal or heart forgiveness, even if your spouse does not repent. We might call the second level transacted or relational forgiveness if your spouse repents (see step 9 below).

The first level is unconditional and involves a heart commitment before God (Mark 11:25; Luke 23:34a). It involves three commitments:

- Releasing your spouse from your judgment and entrusting him or her to God (Romans 12:19; 1 Peter 2:22–23; 4:19)
- Emptying your heart of bitterness (Ephesians 4:31–32)
- Being willing to grant transacted forgiveness and reconcile the relationship if your spouse repents (Matthew 18:12–14 with 18:15–17; Luke 17:3–4)

These commitments don't just happen; you must cultivate them. It will take time for the truths of the gospel to soak into your heart after infidelity. Your flesh will resist the thought of showing mercy toward your spouse. It's one thing to have a right attitude toward God (our previous chapters); it's another to have a right attitude to someone who personally betrayed you.

How can you cultivate such a gracious heart posture? By continually, prayerfully meditating on God's grace to you in Christ and asking God to change your heart. Consider six truths that can prevent bitterness from building up and can move your heart toward a merciful response.[3]

1. *Remember God's enormous love for you displayed on the cross.* As you recognize the multimillion-dollar debt your sin incurred against God and how Christ paid that debt for you, your spouse's sins, though grievous, look different (Matthew 18:21–35). You realize that no one,

including your spouse, has sinned against you as much as you have sinned against God; but God in Christ has completely forgiven you your massive debt. In light of the cross of Jesus, God calls you to "Be kind and compassionate to one another, forgiving each other, just as in Christ God forgave you" (Ephesians 4:32). A growing grasp of the gospel will better enable you to forgive your spouse.

2. *Remember your desperate need for God's forgiveness.* In several places our Lord Jesus connected God's forgiveness of our sins with our forgiveness of others. Mark 11:25 records Jesus's instructions, "And when you stand praying, if you hold anything against anyone, forgive them, so that your Father in heaven may forgive you your sins." In his model prayer for his disciples, Jesus said, "forgive us our debts, as we also have forgiven our debtors. . . . For if you forgive other people when they sin against you, your heavenly Father will also forgive you. But if you do not forgive others their sins, your Father will not forgive your sins" (Matthew 6:12, 14–15; also 18:35). While scholars debate what type of forgiveness God will withhold, none are what we would want to experience. We forgive others because we want to live in the reality of God's forgiveness of us.

3. *Remember your ultimate need for God's mercy.* Jesus highlighted the character of his followers with the fifth beatitude, "Blessed are the merciful, for they will be shown mercy" (Matthew 5:7). God's mercy toward us becomes the motive and model for displaying mercy toward others, even our enemies, "Be merciful, just as your Father is merciful" (Luke 6:36). This theme likely

influenced the apostle James, as he reminds us, "because judgment without mercy will be shown to anyone who has not been merciful. Mercy triumphs over judgment" (James 2:13). You should show mercy to your sinful spouse because God shows you mercy, and your good is in being like God.

4. *Remember God, not you, is the judge.* When we become bitter, we place ourselves in the dangerous role of playing God, assuming his role as the "one Lawgiver and Judge, the one who is able to save and destroy" (James 4:12). Bitter people grab God's throne of judgment. As we saw in the previous chapter, Joseph's merciful response to his brothers in Genesis 50 models his trust in God and in God's sovereignty, wisdom, and goodness. He realizes that he is not in the place of God and refuses to exact revenge (Genesis 50:19–20). You must avoid assuming God's role and instead entrust your unfaithful spouse into God's hands. Let God be angry before you. He does not let sin go unaccounted for. In fact, all sin was or will be punished by God, either through the cross of Christ, who bore the sins of all who will repent and believe in him (John 1:29), or on the day of final judgment for all who don't repent and believe (Hebrews 9:27–28).

5. *Remember the offender's sin involves both disobedience and slavery.* Bitterness reveals an incomplete understanding of the other person's sin. We wrongly assume that malice motivated an unfaithful spouse's every act. We forget that as a sinner, the offender is both responsible for his sin but also deceived and enslaved by his sin (Proverbs 5:22; Luke 23:34; John 8:34; 1 Corinthians

2:8; 2 Peter 2:19). Here's how I previously summarized this dynamic:

> Let me say this delicately, especially if someone sinned against you severely. A Christlike perspective on your offender includes recognizing that person's slavery and self-deception. It means not taking that person's sin against you too personally.
>
> As a pastor and counselor, I have been privileged to help couples restore their marriages after adultery. That has meant interviewing men and women who have been unfaithful to their partner. I have never heard a husband say, "Well, Bob, here's what happened. I woke up one morning and decided on a whim that I wanted to destroy my wife's life. So I thought about it. How should I do it? Hmm, I know. I'll have an affair. Yeah, that's the ticket. Hmm, but with whom? Let me think. I know. I'll go sleep with . . ."
>
> That's not the way it typically happens. Instead, the man pursues his own desires—which he and our culture wrongly call "needs"—desires for control, for power, for affection, for admiration, or for something new, daring, or illicit. Maybe another woman shows him attention. She laughs at his jokes and thinks, *He's so nice.* Gradually—and blindly—he continues down this path until it turns sexual. But ultimately it was not about

his wife's supposed failures, or even about his preference for the other woman. It was about him and his pride and self-centeredness, and demands. His sin enslaved him and blinded him to his God and to his wife.

Please understand. Such a man remains entirely responsible for his decisions. He is rebellious and disobedient. . . . But he is also deceived and enslaved, to be pitied. In fact, one of the spectacular, Godlike turning points for the wife occurs right here: Along with her (understandable) struggle with anger, she begins to feel a surprising measure of Christ-like compassion for this man who betrayed her. She sees how he has blindly followed his own way. She learns not to take his sin too personally, and to see his sin as chiefly not against her but against God. And while she has never committed adultery, she understands that both his adultery and her own multimillion-dollar sins arise from the same selfish root: "We all, like sheep, have gone astray, each of us has turned to his own way; and the LORD has laid on him [Christ] the iniquity of us all" (Isaiah 53:6).

This was the master stroke for Debbie. She came to see that her three years of bitterness were a result of her own three years of blindness. She failed to see Aaron as God saw him. As Debbie's Christian friend helped her to see Aaron properly, and as she encouraged Debbie to talk to her husband, Debbie was able to hear for the first time—with compassion—Aaron's self-deceived struggle with his own sin.[4]

6. *Remember your own fallibility and susceptibility to sin.* Bitterness reveals our pride. We forget that as sinners, we are capable of the same sins as others and that the same root sins may already reside in us. Proverbs 16:18 alerts us to our grave danger: "Pride goes before destruction, a haughty spirit before a fall." The apostle Paul offers the same warning: "If you think you are standing firm, be careful that you don't fall!" (1 Corinthians 10:12). In our bitterness we proudly pretend moral superiority and self-deceived invulnerability. Aware of the power of remaining sin, the writer to the Hebrews reminds the church, "See to it, brothers and sisters, that none of you has a sinful, unbelieving heart that turns away from the living God. But encourage one another daily, as long as it is called 'Today,' so that none of you may be hardened by sin's deceitfulness" (Hebrews 3:12–13). Even professing Christians are not immune from the dangers of a deceitful heart that overlooks its own sin and judges others.

What does this danger look like? It begins with sentiments like these: "I would never do to someone else what he (or she) did to me!" "I can't believe he did that; I would never do that to him!" When we say things like that, surely the Lord winces at such self-confidence. Are you really so sure that you couldn't do that? Maybe you have not been tempted toward infidelity. But have you ever daydreamed about a different spouse or found yourself jealous of another couple? If your spouse's sin was rooted in discontentment, physical desire, rebellion, or boredom, do those themes ever arise in your own heart, even if they take a different behavioral form?

Admittedly, these six gospel implications can be difficult to fathom, especially when viewed all at once. Yet they all stem from Christ's death and resurrection, as his Spirit applies these truths to your heart. Looking at your spouse through the lens of Christ's redemptive work for you will take time, but every minute spent reflecting on God's grace toward you in Christ is well worth it. As you do, you will see heart beliefs and motives shifting toward compassion and mercy and away from rage or revenge, and you will be better prepared to transact forgiveness if he or she does repent.

STEP 7: CONFRONT YOUR SPOUSE TO ENCOURAGE REPENTANCE AND RECONCILIATION

If your spouse has repented, skip this step and move to the next. If not, and if your church hasn't yet confronted your partner, consider taking these steps to confront him or her about the adultery.[5]

To make a confrontation most effective, first answer the following self-examination questions to assess your readiness.[6]

1. Do you have the proper Christlike attitudes, and are you already attitudinally forgiving your spouse in your heart (step 6 above)? Along with the Scripture passages above, review the relational graces in passages like 1 Corinthians

13:4–7; Galatians 5:22–23; Ephesians 4:1–3, 31–32; Colossians 3:12–17; James 3:17–18).

2. Have you confessed your sins to God and your spouse and sought their forgiveness? While you should always confess your sins to God immediately, see step 8 below on when and how to confess your sins to your unrepentant spouse.

3. Do you have the right goal? Do you want to "win" over (Matthew 18:15), "forgive" (Luke 17:3b–4), and "restore . . . gently" (Galatians 6:1), or are you seeking to humiliate or hurt your guilty partner?

4. Do you really believe—are you convinced— that this is the most loving action you can take? While our culture doesn't equate love with rebuke, the Bible does so repeatedly (Leviticus 19:17–18; Proverbs 27:5–6; James 5:19–20). Understanding this step as a loving action will help you resist later accusations from others or even your own conscience.

5. Are you willing to take any or all of the next step(s) that God might require? Passages like Matthew 18:15–17 can guide you and your counselors if your spouse is unrepentant.

6. Are you seeking to please and fear God more than people? Scripture warns us about this (Psalm 56:3–4; Proverbs 29:25; John 12:42–43), and this fear can keep us from properly rebuking those who sin against us.

7. Are you praying for the Spirit's help in approaching your spouse, and for your spouse to be willing to receive your rebuke and repent? Only

the Lord can make your confrontation effective
and change your spouse's heart. Ask the Lord
to grant your spouse true faith and repentance.
8. Do you first need further biblical counsel about
these matters? Be sure to discuss this with your
counselors.

I realize this list might seem overwhelming and
unattainable. But remember that each item can increase
the likelihood of your spouse repenting. And remember that our Lord promises—as we have seen throughout this book—to be with you each moment and to help
you do what he calls you to do.

As the sinned-against partner, you can't control
your spouse's behavior after the adultery. Instead, you
can pray for your spouse, ask the Lord to give you
opportunities to graciously encourage repentance, and
suggest he or she seek the help of a pastor or biblical
counselor. You will be tempted regularly to question
what your spouse is now thinking or doing, whether
repentance will happen, and if you will ever be able to
trust him or her again.

STEP 8: DEAL BIBLICALLY WITH YOUR SINS IN THE MARRIAGE

As we noted earlier, nothing you did caused your
spouse to cheat on you. Your partner's infidelity is not
your fault; he or she remains fully responsible for those
choices. Even if your spouse, your spouse's friends, or
some family member blames you, you can and should
reject their accusations. He or she violated the marriage
covenant; you did not.

At the same time, this doesn't mean you were sin-less or that your sins didn't contribute to (though not cause) the marital problems that might have occasioned your spouse's unfaithfulness. Since your goal in life must be to please God, then drawing near to him to deal with your own sin first must always be a prior-ity, no matter how your spouse acts. The apostle Paul provides a model for us, "So I strive always to keep my conscience clear before God and man" (Acts 24:16).

I realize this step might be difficult. Some of you might be able to see, repent of, and confess your mar-ital sins immediately, in some cases even before your spouse confesses the adultery. In those cases, this step 8 might even be combined with step 7—your confession first, and then your confrontation. But for most people, it will probably take more time to come to grips with what has happened and to process it with the Lord before you are ready to address your sins. Ideally, your unfaithful spouse will confess first, making it easier to confess whatever ways you have fallen short as a spouse.

What does this step entail? It begins with identify-ing ways you have sinned.[7] Our Lord prioritizes this in Matthew 7:3–5,

> "Why do you look at the speck of sawdust in your brother's eye and pay no attention to the plank in your own eye? How can you say to your brother, 'Let me take the speck out of your eye,' when all the time there is a plank in your own eye? You hypocrite, first take the plank out of your own eye, and then you

will see clearly to remove the speck from your brother's eye."

Two lessons emerge from this passage. First, Jesus calls you to prioritize dealing with your sins: "first, take the plank out of your own eye." He exposes our tendency to focus on the sins of others before our own. Second, he calls us to view our sins as more serious than the other person's by calling ours a "plank" and theirs a "speck." While your husband or wife sinned severely against you, before the Lord you must *look upon* your sins in one sense as more serious, because they are primarily against God, and act accordingly. This doesn't mean that your sins before or after your spouse's infidelity were worse in some objective sense than your spouse's (recall chapter 2). It does mean, as you humbly commune with your Lord, that you should *view* your sins as if they were worse.

Before proceeding, however, as mentioned above, you should decide if you are ready for this self-examination step. It might be premature if you haven't sufficiently (albeit, not perfectly) worked through steps 1–6. Instead, you might find it helpful to review those steps and to talk with the Lord. Remember God's presence with you and his promises for you.

Moreover, if you are tempted to believe that anything you did somehow caused your spouse's betrayal, then you should pause. Remember, as we have said repeatedly throughout this book, your behavior did *not* cause your spouse's sin. Discuss this step 8 with your counselors. Identifying and confessing your sins before the Lord and your spouse might be too difficult right now. Remember that you are in-process; your loving Savior is seeking to lead you one step at a time.

If you are ready, however, what steps should you take?[8] First, ask the Lord to search your heart and bring to the surface any sinful attitudes, words, or actions against your spouse (sins of commission) as well as ways you failed to love and serve him or her properly (sins of omission). Scripture doesn't limit sin to willful, deliberate choices; sin is part of our remaining heart condition. Pay special attention to anything that might have made it easier for your spouse to commit or justify infidelity. Consider offenses against him or her before, during, or after the adultery. Pray with David the closing words of Psalm 139:23–24,

> Search me, God, and know my heart;
>> test me and know my anxious thoughts.
> See if there is any offensive way in me,
>> and lead me in the way everlasting.

Second, list those sins and share that list with your biblical counseling team. Invite them to help you clarify those items and even to suggest other items that you might be blind to, based on their caring knowledge of you and the situation.

Third, if you haven't done so, be sure to confess your sins to God and to seek his forgiveness and power to enable you to grow and change. Believe the gospel: "If we confess our sins, he is faithful and just and will forgive us our sins and purify us from all unrighteousness" (1 John 1:9). And run to Jesus Christ: "Let us then approach God's throne of grace with confidence, so that we may receive mercy and find grace to help us in our time of need" (Hebrews 4:16). His grace always infinitely outweighs your sin.

Fourth, seek an opportunity, with the help of your counselors and at the proper time, to confess to your spouse the sins the Lord has convicted you of and to seek forgiveness. This step best occurs as part of the marital counseling or mediation process so a skilled counselor or mediator can guide you both.

For one woman, this fourth step happened in a counseling session. The counselors had worked individually with each partner but occasionally brought them together. In one of those conjoint sessions, she voiced to Andrew (1) that she took no responsibility for his adultery, (2) that the Lord has helped her find strength and hope from him, (3) that the Lord was slowly shifting her heart from anger to mercy, (4) that she awaited a more thorough repentance (part of the understood counseling agenda) beyond his initial admission of his adultery, and (5) that she was praying for him daily. Then she added a sixth component:

> At the same time, the Lord had convicted me of some specific ways I have failed to be the wife the Lord wanted me to be. I want to ask you to forgive me for my various anger outbursts in recent months and for ways I sometimes prioritized my friends over you. None of this, as I have said, excuses what you have done, but I am asking you to forgive me for those sins and, with God's help, I look forward

to working on those areas at the proper time, if the Lord restores our marriage.

As noted earlier, in some cases, you might wisely defer such a confession until after your betraying spouse first repents and seeks forgiveness. In other cases, a more immediate confession might help encourage your spouse to confess his or her adultery. Your counselors can guide you on that decision.

This step of godly self-examination, seeking counsel, confessing to the Lord, and confessing to your spouse brings several benefits. It's an opportunity to please God, clear your conscience before God and others, model humility before your spouse, and give him or her the opportunity to forgive you and move toward reconciliation.

QUESTIONS FOR REFLECTION OR DISCUSSION

1. As you contemplate steps 6, 7, and 8, which do you find most difficult? Why?

2. How do God's promises provide you with the desire and the ability to carry out his counsel? What specific promise or passage of Scripture will enable you to take these steps? (You might want to review chapter 3.)

Chapter 6

RESPONDING WISELY TO YOUR SPOUSE'S DECISION

As we come to this point in the process, I assume that you or your church has confronted your spouse, and he or she has chosen to repent of the infidelity, follow Christ, and recommit to your marriage. If so, then step 9 is God's path for you. (If not, then go to Step 10).

STEP 9: IF YOUR SPOUSE REPENTS, GRANT TRANSACTED FORGIVENESS AND COMMIT TO REBUILDING YOUR MARRIAGE

As the heading notes, this step of forgiveness comes "if" your spouse repents. This requires you, your counselors, and the church to collectively assess the reality of your spouse's change. Scripture distinguishes between true and false repentance, inward change (that produces outward change) and outward-only change, and godly and worldly sorrow. While evaluating repentance is beyond the scope of this book, credible repentance involves a thorough confession by your spouse of his or her sins against God and you, a complete severance of the adulterous relationship, renewed humility and love toward you, and an evident godly change in speech and actions. Passages like Psalms 32; 51; 2 Corinthians 7:10–11; Galatians 5:22–23; and James 3:13–18 can guide you and your team in making that assessment. Of course, only the Lord can see the heart, so you must trust him to care for you even if your spouse's seemingly credible repentance later proves false.

If, however, the Lord has brought you and your spouse this far in the process, be encouraged and give him praise. The kind of repentance and faith that your husband or wife is now exhibiting is a miraculous gift from God.

Granting transacted forgiveness

In step 6 above, we distinguished two levels of forgiveness. We considered the first level unconditional, attitudinal forgiveness even if your spouse was not repentant. This involved releasing your spouse from your judgment and entrusting him or her to God as judge, repenting of bitterness, and being willing to grant transacted forgiveness and reconcile the relationship if the offender repents.

What, then, does the second level—transacted (or granted or relational) forgiveness—entail? Like God, in response to your spouse's credible confession and repentance, you decide to forgive. You declare to your spouse your forgiveness, and you make three promises.[1]

First, you promise not to dwell on your spouse's sin. While you cannot control what memories might invade your mind, you can promise to deal biblically with them when they do arise. You can ask the Lord to guard your heart, and you can remind yourself of the gospel truths in step 6 above and the promise you have made. The invasion of unwanted memories doesn't mean you haven't forgiven your partner, only that you need God's ongoing help to renew that commitment.

Second, you promise to not mention your spouse's sin to other people. You are deciding to not gossip. This doesn't mean you can't seek counseling from a confidential biblical counselor if you need ongoing help. And it doesn't mean you and your spouse together can't share your story with those who need to know, or to forge a testimony of God's redeeming grace in your marriage. But it does mean you will not share any information that might hurt your spouse. You are promising to do good, not evil, to your spouse with your words.

Third, you promise to not bring up your spouse's sin, use it against him or her, or let it hinder your relationship. Love, as 1 Corinthians 13:5 observes, "keeps no record of wrongs." When God forgives us, he moves toward us, embraces us, and holds nothing against us. As Hebrews 8:12 declares, "For I will forgive their wickedness and will remember their sins no more." With his help, you can treat your repentant partner in similar ways.

In a previous book, I described my saddest and most glaring counseling counterexample:

The husband had committed adultery years prior. As I learned about the incident in our first session, they assured me that they had resolved the past, that confession and forgiveness had occurred, and that any current problems were unrelated. But I wondered. In one session they argued back and forth over a seemingly minor matter, blaming each other, until she played the forbidden trump card: "Yeah, but at least I wasn't the one who cheated on you." The discussion ended as he left the room in rage. She sat there with her head in her hands, angry at him but more angry at herself. The past was not properly restored. It took several sessions to unpack the past infidelity and lead them both, for the first time, to true confession, true forgiveness, and true marital unity.[2]

Your spouse's repentance and your three forgiveness promises can become a vital turning point in the process and allow you both to move forward to restore your marriage. This doesn't mean you won't face temptations—sometimes strong ones—to revisit the offense. As we have seen throughout the book, your strong, ever-present Savior can help you fight against the temptation to re-dwell on your spouse's sin. It does mean you have established a standard to return to when you are tempted to fixate on his or her past infidelity and you have a referent point to begin to move forward in restoring the relationship.

At this point, however, you may encounter a significant struggle that many people in your situation face.

It might be your biggest obstacle. Even if you are able to forgive your partner and renew the three promises as needed, the fear of him or her repeating that sin might haunt you. Here's what it sounds like: "I can forgive my spouse; I just need to know it will never happen again." No desire is more natural than that.

Here's the pastoral counsel I've given to sinned-against wives (or sinned-against husbands) in these cases:

> My friend, your struggle makes total sense to me. Unfortunately, no one can make that guarantee to you. While your husband's repentance seems sincere and he and the church have in place a sound plan of accountability for him and counseling for your marriage, not even he can know with absolute certainty he won't fall. None of us knows the depth and danger of our remaining sin, not to mention the powerful temptations presented by Satan and the sinful world around us. Paul's admonition against such arrogance remains true: "So, if you think you are standing firm, be careful that you don't fall!" (1 Cor. 10:12).[3]
>
> Part of me so wants you to have this guarantee, to assure you that your husband will never do it again. I feel the heartbreak you have suffered and the pain you have endured. But the other part of me doesn't want you to have that guarantee even if I could give it. Why not? Because I don't want your faith dependent on your husband's fidelity but on God's fidelity. I

don't want you to build your life on anything that God has not guaranteed.

Sometimes, when people fear the future possibility of some dreadful thing, they say, "well, we'll cross that bridge if we come to it." I'd like to revise that saying: If you come to that bridge—if your spouse were to become unfaithful again—*you* will not cross that bridge. Instead, you *and your Lord Jesus* will cross that bridge, together. And I and our church will walk with you and the Lord. So, I can't guarantee it won't happen, but I can guarantee Jesus Christ will be with you. Find your ultimate assurance in him.

In other words, recalling chapter 1 above, make sure your capital-H Hope is in the Lord and don't build your life on even the most understandable small-h hopes. Growth in Christ for you will involve continually submitting to the Lord these legitimate desires for marital fidelity. Fearing God rightly will reorient all your other fears.

Rebuilding your marriage

As exciting as your spouse's repentance and your ability to forgive him or her might be, it isn't the end of the process; it's a renewed beginning. Stress points existed before the betrayal; the adultery didn't happen in a vacuum. Moreover, sins were likely committed during the period of alienation. The emotional high and the newfound marital inertia you each might feel now typically won't remain at that level. Even so-called make-up sex might bring an initial thrill, especially if you have not been together since the discovery or disclosure of the infidelity, but you might have previous or new sexual problems to address. If you have been living separately during the reconciliation process, then you and your spouse might have begun to form separate habits. And your pre-adultery communication problems and relational conflicts won't evaporate simply by reconciling the adultery. Much marital work is needed. Rebuilding trust will take months and even years of mutual Christian growth, as your spouse demonstrates the ongoing fruit of repentance, and you continually entrust your life and marriage to the Lord. You will need patience and perseverance.

But here's the good news: God stands ready by his Spirit to help you. Do you believe that? Jesus can not only restore your marriage but make it stronger than it was before. We don't want to merely revert to the pre-infidelity state of your marriage. In Christ, God provides something better. Here's why: Our God delights in making broken things better than they were. Like a severed steel joint made strong by the welding process, the Redeemer can weld your severed marriage into something sturdy. The lives of many "welded" couples attest to this. The God of new birth, new life, and new beginnings offers something more than restoration; he offers transformation.[4] Contrary to some people's opinion, adultery alone does not destroy a Christian marriage; only unbelief, unrepentance, and unforgiveness do.

If for some reason you haven't been guided by a pastor or a biblical counselor working under your pastor, as we advised in chapter 1, please pursue that help now. While not every marriage conflict requires a biblical counselor, this one does. It takes a skilled counselor to help you rebuild your marriage after adultery. You will each need to address both your individual and marital sins—on both the heart (root) and the behavior (fruit) levels—that both precipitated and attended the betrayal. You might also need to address other dynamics involving past and present suffering. All this requires a skilled, thorough, biblical counseling process. (Note: I tell my marriage counseling students that only now will *marriage* counseling begin; prior to this it's been separate ministries to someone who has sinned in serious ways and someone who has been sinned against.)

STEP 10: IF YOUR SPOUSE DOESN'T REPENT, DEMONSTRATE CHRISTLIKE LOVE AND MERCY

Unfortunately, as we said in chapter 1, you might do everything God wants you to do—the steps laid out in this book—yet find your spouse remains unrepentant with no small-h hope for marital restoration. He or she might be angry, hostile, defensive, cold, unresponsive, or avoidant. Either way, your spouse shows no godly sorrow or commitment to reconcile with you.

What should you do? Our Lord's counsel in Luke 6:27–36 provides the basis for a biblical game plan for how to love your enemies,[5] a plan you can apply in dealing with your unrepentant spouse.

"But to you who are listening I say: Love your enemies, do good to those who hate you, bless

those who curse you, pray for those who mis-
treat you. If someone slaps you on one cheek,
turn to them the other also. If someone takes
your coat, do not withhold your shirt from
them. Give to everyone who asks you, and
if anyone takes what belongs to you, do not
demand it back. Do to others as you would
have them do to you. If you love those who love
you, what credit is that to you? Even sinners
love those who love them. And if you do good
to those who are good to you, what credit is
that to you? Even sinners do that. And if you
lend to those from whom you expect repay-
ment, what credit is that to you? Even sinners
lend to sinners, expecting to be repaid in full.
But love your enemies, do good to them, and
lend to them without expecting to get anything
back. Then your reward will be great, and you
will be children of the Most High, because he
is kind to the ungrateful and wicked. Be merciful, just as your Father is merciful."

The passage is a distinct unit bookended by the
call to love (v. 27) and to be merciful (v. 36), two Bible
mega-words summarizing our duty to others. What do
love and mercy toward an enemy look like in practice?
The rest of verses 27–28 give three broad categories: we
must do good to, bless, and pray for our enemies. Verses
29–35 give specific examples of these three categories.

To apply this passage in your situation, begin by
asking the Lord to give you a heart of love and mercy
toward your spouse. Then draw three columns with

the words *Do Good, Bless/Speak*, and *Pray* on top. (I'm broadening the term *bless* to include godly speaking.) Brainstorm specific ways you might do good to, speak well to or about, and pray for yourself and your partner. Getting advice from your counseling team will help.

But one roadblock remains in our model. What power will enable you to do good, speak well, and pray for your spouse, not only after what he or she has done (adultery), but also after what he or she has not done (repent)? Review verses 35–36. Jesus assures you that a "great reward" awaits you, even if the other person never reconciles with you, and you will show yourself to be "children of the Most High," like your Father who is "kind" and "merciful" even to the "ungrateful and wicked." "Be merciful," says our Lord, "just as your Father is merciful."

To carry out our Lord's game plan—to demonstrate love and mercy toward your unrepentant partner—you must grasp God's love, kindness, and mercy toward his enemies. But lest you wrongly think of God's enemies as some group of "really bad guys out there, somewhere," remember how Romans 5:6–11 describes people like you and me: we were powerless, ungodly, sinners, and enemies of God.

So, if you find it difficult to do what Jesus tells you to do to your enemies, remember what he did for you while you were once his enemy and let that truth increasingly reorient your beliefs, motives, and affections. I know various betrayed wives and husbands who understood these Bible truths but struggled to reflect God's love, kindness, and mercy, and to do good, bless, and pray for their unrepentant spouse. But as

they communed with Christ through the personal (e.g.,
Bible reading and prayer) and corporate (e.g., worship
and fellowship) means of grace, he progressively trans-
formed them.

For example, Tara found her bitterness toward
unrepentant Michael slowly shift from her being
betrayed to her deepening sadness over his rebellious
state and his desperate need for God's grace. She testi-
fied, "I was livid when I learned Michael had cheated on
me, but I never anticipated what the Lord would do in
my life through this trial." The Lord used four specific
factors to help Tara. First, her pastor's sermons on Ephesians 1–2, and some follow-up conversations with him,
helped her grasp her richly blessed state as God's daughter. Second, her counselor used the above Luke 6 model
to guide her in some practical choices about what she
should say to him. Third, a caring Christian sister met
and prayed with Tara several times each week, bringing
the presence of Christ to her. And fourth, the Sunday
worship services, including the hymns (e.g., "How Firm
a Foundation") and prayers, helped stabilize her soul
amid her emotional turbulence. God's Spirit used God's
Word in the presence of God's people to transform Tara.

We'll close this chapter by briefly discussing three
common questions concerning your relationship with
your unrepentant spouse, although some questions
might apply in every adultery situation. Before con-
sidering any of these, please talk with your pastors and
your counseling team.

First, may you separate from your spouse? Most
Bible-believing churches and biblical counselors not
only support but encourage a short-term, structured,

goal-oriented marital separation in cases of adultery. Such a separation gives space to each partner and allows individual counseling and between-session growth assignments, with the goal of relational reconciliation and marital restoration where possible. While many variables might dictate the specific timetable, the separation might involve a month or two at a time, to be renewed as needed, as the parties and their counselors assess each person's progress.

Second, may you divorce your spouse? Again, you should discuss this question with your pastor since biblical Christians differ on these matters.[6] I and most evangelical pastors and biblical counselors view divorce as permissible in cases of sexual immorality (Matthew 5:31–32; 19:9), so we would not oppose or discipline a spouse who chose that path. However, this might or might not be best for your soul or be what God wants you to do. If your spouse demonstrates credible repentance, it might be best, with the help of your pastor and counselors, to pursue not only relational reconciliation (forgiveness) but full marital restoration (with ongoing marital counseling). If, however, your spouse remains unrepentant after a significant amount of time (a judgment call best made in consultation with your pastor and counselors), especially after you make the efforts outlined in this book, then divorcing an unrepentant spouse might be the most loving action you can take— to serve as a wake-up call for your spouse's soul and to keep him or her from making a further mockery of the sacred covenant of marriage.

Third, should your church be involved in disciplining your unrepentant spouse? Here nearly every

Bible-believing pastor would say yes.[7] While any unre-
pented sin could subject a church member to the kind of
formal, corrective discipline described in passages like
Matthew 18:15–20 and 1 Corinthians 5, the severity of
adultery should make this need obvious. Without true
repentance, this would eventually lead to excommuni-
cation. If your church hasn't confronted your spouse
and initiated this process, then speak to your pastor,
since discipline displays God's love to your spouse and
functions as one of God's primary means of grace to
restore your spouse to God and to you. In many cases,
it's best to wait for your church to carry out their disci-
plinary steps before initiating the divorce process.

Yet, whether you stay married or divorce, and
whether your church does or doesn't discipline your
spouse, the truths about loving your enemy from Luke 6
can still guide your attitudes and actions and your relationship with your unrepentant spouse or ex-spouse.

QUESTIONS FOR REFLECTION OR DISCUSSION

1. In one sense, the choice between steps 9 and 10
   depends on your spouse being repentant (step 9) or
   not repentant (step 10). But in another sense, the two
   scenarios share commonalities. What attitudes and
   actions are proper for you to demonstrate whether
   your spouse is or isn't repentant?

2. As you finish reading this book and walking
   through its ten steps, how would you describe any
   change in perspective you have experienced? What
   new insights have you gained? What old truths

have become renewed for you? Share this with your counselor(s).

3. How has this journey given you a ministry vision to help others who suffer what you have? Remember "the God and Father of our Lord Jesus Christ, the Father of compassion and the God of all comfort, who comforts us in all our troubles, so that we can comfort those in any trouble with the comfort we ourselves receive from God" (2 Corinthians 1:3–5).

Conclusion

MOVING FORWARD WITH YOUR LORD

As you can see, we've covered a lot of ground. We've explored the dynamics of betrayal, and we've done work in our own hearts before the Lord. We have reflected on Scripture and let God's Word comfort and convict us. We've sought outside help and counsel from others. Our ten-step reading journey is now ending, but your ten-step implementation of this biblical counsel will continue. But no book, especially a short one, can give you detailed guidance that is particular to you, your spouse, the adultery, and many other variables. Yet the presence, power, and promises of the Lord are particular to you. He speaks to you in his Word, as his Spirit leads you to follow Jesus, and as his people (the church) minister to you and provide wise, compassionate care.

We close with two final pieces of counsel that will apply to you no matter what your spouse does or whatever happens to your marriage.

THE PROCESS NATURE IN MOVING FORWARD

First, realize that your ongoing growth will take time. Christian growth in general, and rebuilding your life and marriage after adultery in particular, involves a process. Theologians call this progressive sanctification. Expect that you will need to review and repeat the ten steps we have covered:

Step 1: Believe God is powerfully present with you to help you.

Step 2: Cry out to God for help.

Step 3: Recognize your core identity as God's son or daughter, not your spouse's husband or wife.

Step 4: Seek to obey and please God, no matter what.

Step 5: Embrace God's sovereign, wise, loving purposes in your suffering.

Step 6: Cultivate a heart of mercy and attitudinal forgiveness.

Step 7: Confront your spouse and encourage him or her to repent and follow Christ.

Step 8: Deal biblically with your contributions to the marriage problems.

Step 9: If your spouse repents, grant transacted forgiveness and commit to rebuilding your marriage.

Step 10: If your spouse doesn't repent, demonstrate Christlike love and mercy.

You should prepare for periodic and sometimes intense memory invasions—unwelcomed and uninvited—even if your partner has repented and sought your forgiveness. Such memories will not go away immediately and may never completely in this life. Your anger might flare up, even after you have forgiven your partner. If so, seize these occasions as rich opportunities to trust in the Lord, to remember the cross and resurrection of your Lord Jesus, and to renew your previous promises to forgive. God's Spirit, in time, can redeem those memories for God's glory and your good.

You will also be tempted to doubt your spouse's fidelity, become unduly suspicious, or even spy on him or her. Without being naïve and forsaking whatever specific accountability role that you, your spouse, and your counselors agree you should play, you will need daily, even moment-to-moment help from the Lord. You will need to *trust* the Lord to do for you what he has promised you in his Word and to *entrust* your spouse to the Lord to do whatever the Lord wills in your spouse's life.

YOUR LIFE IN CHRIST IS MORE THAN YOUR MARRIAGE

Doubtless the events surrounding your spouse's infidelity have consumed you, and you have felt a myriad of swirling emotions. Dozens of questions, along with fears and frustrations, fill your mind.

Thankfully, Scripture gives a bigger vision of the Christian life:

> Since, then, you have been raised with Christ,
> set your hearts on things above, where Christ
> is, seated at the right hand of God. Set your
> minds on things above, not on earthly things.
> For you died, and your life is now hidden with
> Christ in God. (Colossians 3:1–3)

Being raised and hidden with Christ and having your heart and mind set on the things of Christ means that your life is more than your marriage. You have a personal relationship with Christ to cultivate and an inner life to develop. You have friends and fellow church members to minister to and spiritual gifts to exercise. You might have parents and children to serve. You have a job to perform and income to generate. You have a body to steward and housing and possessions to manage. You have unsaved friends, family, and neighbors to evangelize. You have civic duties as a citizen to render. While your marriage remains an important part of your life, it's only a part. Even if all these things ceased, living with and for Jesus outweighs them all.

To help you not be consumed by your spouse's adultery, let's close with a final passage that pictures this bigger vision. In Psalm 73, after a crisis of faith nearly led Asaph to throw away his faith, God revealed himself in a way that dramatically steeled Asaph's soul. In the closing section Asaph records his newfound confidence:

> Yet I am always with you;
>   you hold me by my right hand.

> You guide me with your counsel,
>> and afterward you will take me into glory.
>>> (vv. 23–24)

For you, this means the Lord is with you, the Lord holds you, the Lord guides you with his Word, and the Lord will take you to be with him forever in heaven. He provides you with your best life now and forever. At times your prayers might simply be, "Lord, be near me. Lord, hold me, Lord guide me." And he will.

These truths gripped Asaph's soul. He continues in verse 25, "Whom have I in heaven but you? And earth has nothing I desire besides you." No one and no thing—including your husband or wife—can compare to God and provide true stability and satisfaction, even when doubts arise: "My flesh and my heart may fail, but God is the strength of my heart and my portion forever" (v. 26). God is all that Asaph needed and all you need in this life and in the life to come.

The psalmist then ends with another gripping contrast:

> Those who are far from you will perish;
>> you destroy all who are unfaithful to you.
> But as for me, it is good to be near God.
>> I have made the Sovereign Lord my refuge;
>> I will tell of all your deeds. (vv. 27–28)

Among the many small-h hopes you might desire or imagine, God wants drawing near to him to be your ultimate good and your strongest refuge. Let no husband or wife or any other person or relationship supplant the preeminence of your God—Father, Son, and

Holy Spirit. He remains your capital-H Hope when your spouse is faithful or unfaithful.

My dear brother or sister, while our ten-step reading journey is now ending, your application of this biblical counsel will continue. But what will also continue is the presence, power, and promises of your Lord. He speaks to you in his Word. His Spirit comforts you and leads you to trust and follow Jesus. And his people (the church) minister to you and provide you with wise, compassionate care. His grace in all its fullness goes before you.

As we close, let this final truth capture you: All that the Lord has done, is doing, and will do for you and in you is preparing you for another wedding day, described at the end of our Bible as "the wedding supper of the Lamb" (Revelation 19:6–9). On that day, you and I and all his people will live forever in the presence of our faithful Savior, Jesus Christ, the one who will never leave us or forsake us.

ENDNOTES

Chapter 1

1. Portions of this book have been adapted from my minibook, *Restoring Your Broken Marriage: Healing after Adultery* (Greensboro, NC: New Growth Press, 2009), an earlier, shorter work that briefly addresses both the offended and the offender. I also recommend Winston T. Smith, *Help! My Spouse Committed Adultery: First Steps for Dealing with Betrayal* (Greensboro, NC: New Growth Press, 2008).

2. Jones, *Restoring Your Broken Marriage*, 26.

3. The names in each case vignette are pseudonyms and often composites of various people I have counseled over many decades in various churches.

4. For the truths about the Spirit in this paragraph, see Romans 8:9, 15; 1 Corinthians 6:19; Galatians 4:6; 2 Timothy 1:14.

Chapter 2

1. This list has been adapted and expanded from Jones, *Restoring Your Broken Marriage*, 3.

2. For help in distinguishing righteous and sinful anger, see Robert D. Jones, *Uprooting Anger: Biblical Help for a Common Problem* (Phillipsburg, NJ: P&R Publishing, 2005), 27–44.

3. For a fuller discussion of what we might distinguish between clear guilt and confused guilt, see Robert D. Jones, "Understanding Guilt, Repentance, and Forgiveness," in

Robert D. Jones, Kristin L. Kellen, and Rob Green, *The Gospel for Disordered Lives: An Introduction to Christ-Centered Biblical Counseling* (Nashville: B&H Academic, 2021), 84–86.

Chapter 3

1. Jones, *Restoring Your Broken Marriage*, 5.

Chapter 4

1. For a helpful discussion of this matter from a biblical-theological perspective, with practical implications, see Donald A. Carson, *How Long, O Lord? Reflections on Suffering and Evil*, rev. ed. (Grand Rapids: Baker, 2006), especially chapter 17, "The Mystery of Providence," 177–203.

2. See Carson, 180–81, for more examples.

3. Adapted from Robert D. Jones, *When Trouble Shows Up: Seeing God's Transforming Love* (Greensboro, NC: New Growth Press, 2013), which provides a fuller treatment, including supporting Bible passages and examples.

4. Jones, *Restoring Your Broken Marriage*, 19.

Chapter 5

1. Throughout this chapter, I will recommend specific sections in Robert D. Jones, *Pursuing Peace: A Christian Guide to Handling Our Conflicts* (Wheaton, IL: Crossway, 2012), which explains and illustrates each topic in greater detail. Taken and adapted from *Pursuing Peace* by Robert D. Jones, Copyright © 2012, pp. 163, 76–88, 122–36, 159–60, 162–64. Used by permission of Crossway, a publishing ministry of Good News Publishers, Wheaton, IL 60187, www.crossway.org.

2. Adapted from Jones, *Pursuing Peace*, 122–36.

3. The six headings have been adapted from Robert D. Jones, *Freedom from Resentment: Stopping Hurts from Turning Bitter* (Greensboro, NC: New Growth Press, 2010), 7–26.

4. Jones, *Freedom from Resentment*, 21–24.

5. For further help, see Jones, *Pursuing Peace*, 151–66.

6. Adapted from Jones, *Pursuing Peace*, 159–60.

7. Adapted from Jones, *Pursuing Peace*, 76–82.

8. Adapted from Jones, *Pursuing Peace*, 83–88.

Chapter 6

1. Adapted from Jones, *Pursuing Peace*, 162–64.

2. Jones, *Pursuing Peace*, 163.

3. Adapted from Jones, *Pursuing Peace*, 164.

4. Adapted from Jones, *Restoring Your Broken Marriage*, 9.

5. Adapted from Jones, *Pursuing Peace*, 187–92. For further help on dealing with those who won't reconcile, including a fuller exposition and application of this passage, see chapter 12 in Jones, *Pursuing Peace*. See also Romans 12:17–21; 1 Peter 2:21–25; 4:19.

6. For a helpful resource that reflects the majority view of evangelical pastors and biblical counselors, see Jim Newheiser, *Marriage, Divorce, and Remarriage: Critical Questions and Answers* (Phillipsburg, NJ: P&R Publishing, 2017).

7. For a helpful resource on church discipline, see Jay E. Adams, *Handbook for Church Discipline* (Grand Rapids, MI: Zondervan, 1986).

ASK THE CHRISTIAN COUNSELOR

The Ask the Christian Counselor series from New Growth Press is a series of compact books featuring biblical counseling answers to many of life's common problems. This series walks readers through their deepest and most profound questions. Each question is unpacked by an experienced counselor, who gives readers the tools to understand their struggle and to see how the gospel brings hope and healing to the problem they are facing.

Each book in the series is longer than our popular minibooks, but still short enough not to overwhelm the reader. These books can be read by individuals on their own or used within a counseling setting.

NewGrowthPress.com